Statistics from the Very Beginning

Guide in Examples

Mark Smart

Keywords: statistics for beginners, statistics for data science, linear regression, statistical inference, binomial distribution, statistics book, statistical learning, kurtosis, skewness.

Table of Contents

Disclaimer

While all attempts have been made to verify the information provided in this book, the author does assume any responsibility for errors, omissions, or contrary interpretations of the subject matter contained within. The information provided in this book is for educational and entertainment purposes only. The reader is responsible for his or her own actions and the author does not accept any responsibilities for any liabilities or damages, real or perceived, resulting from the use of this information.

The trademarks that are used are without any consent, and the publication of the trademark is without permission or backing by the trademark owner. All trademarks and brands within this book are for clarifying purposes only and are the owned by the owners themselves, not affiliated with this document.

Introduction

Most people know statistics as a good way of describing data. What they don't know is that statistics is a good way of making predictions. It can be seen as solving problems using data. Data is very rich. With a proper analysis of data, we can gain a lot of information. This information can be good for decision making purposes in businesses, organizations and companies. Relying on statistics means that we will make evidence-based decisions rather than relying on our own intuitions which might be wrong. We only need to gather enough data, analyze it via statistical means then make predictions.

There are chances of being wrong when making predictions. Statistics takes this into consideration by quantifying the amount of error we might make. This way, we are able to get new information that was not known before. Statistics is a very broad field and applicable in various fields including academics, data science and others. This book is an excellent guide for you to understand statistics. Enjoy reading!

Chapter 1- Basic Definitions

Discrete vs. Continuous variables

Discrete variables can include numbers that are decimals waiting on the variables that you are using. Suppose you are talking about medical procedures. It is impossible for you to have 3.6793182 medical procedures in a real life. This will never happen even if it is the average. We can either have 3 or 4. With discrete variables, we can create a tabular presentation of the data. For example:

- $1 - 20\%$
- $2 - 30\%$
- $4 - 20\%$

The above data could be a representation of the probability of having a particular number of medical procedures in a year.

However, with continuous variables, it is impossible to present them in a visual manner as above. With continuous variables, we reference them using a formula since we may have infinite variables. Examples of continuous variables include age, weight etc. You are not only 26 years old, but 26 years old, 200 days, 2 hours, 4 seconds, 1 millisecond and the chain continuous.

This can be any moment in time and every interval has some infinite intervals inside it.

Categorical vs. Nominal Variable

A qualitative data is usually referred to as categorical data. Categorical data is simply data that may be added into their respective categories depending on their characteristics. A nominal variable has either two or more categories, and these categories have no implied ordering. Here are examples of nominal variables:

- Gender - Male, Female

- Marital Status - Married, Unmarried, Divorcee

- State - Texas, Haryana, Michigan, Illinois

An ordinal variable has either two or more categories, and these have a very clear ordering. Here are examples of ordinal variables:

- Scale - Strongly Agree, Agree, Neutral, Disagree, Strongly Disagree,

- Rating - Very low, Low, Medium, Great, Very great

An interval variable is the same as an ordinal variable, but the intervals between the interval variable values are spaced equally. This means that an interval variable has order as well as equal intervals.

A good example is when measuring temperature in Celsius. A temperature of 40 degrees Celsius is higher than that of 30 degrees Celsius, while a temperature of 20 degrees Celsius is higher than that of 10 degrees Celsius.

As you can see, we have used a common interval of 10 from one measure of temperature to another.

A ratio is an interval data having a natural zero point. When the value of the variable is 0.0, it is means that there is none of the variable. Here are examples of ratio variables:

- Height

- Weight

- Temperature measured in Kelvin – this is a ratio variable since 0.0 Kelvin in real sense means there is no temperature.

Chapter 2-Significance Testing

Suppose you have some data and you are asked to determine the credibility of a particular statement regarding the population. With statistical significance, one is able to evaluate whether the likelihood of an observed difference is as a result of chance.

Independent T-Test

This type of test is good for checking whether a means for two independent groups have a significant difference between each other. Note that this type of test can only be applied for 2 groups of samples. In case you are having more than two groups, then it is recommended that you use ANOVA.

The following are the assumptions when carrying out an independent T-Test:

1. Every score is sampled randomly and independently.

2. The scores are distributed with the two groups.

3. All the groups have an equal variance.

Significance tests are very important in statistics. Through a significance test, researchers are able to know whether their data rejects or supports their null hypothesis. It also helps them know whether they should accept the alternative hypothesis.

P-value and Significance Level

Significance refers to the relationship between two important quantities, the significance level (alpha) and p-value. A result can be termed as statistically significant when P < alpha. Let us discuss each of these two quantities:

1. p-value- This quantity is calculated after obtaining the results. It refers to the probability of observing extreme effect even when the null hypothesis is still true. The most important thing to note about this is that it doesn't measure the size of the effect.

2. alpha- this I determined before data is gathered. It is the probability of a study rejecting a null hypothesis despite the hypothesis being true (this is the probability of Type 1 error). It is a very important error rate and usually set to a value below 5%.

You should note that there is nothing inherent with the 5% confidence level. It is simply a popular convention. The best point to set the threshold at is determined by the data in use and the goal the researchers are trying to achieve.

Sciences in which the natural variation and random error re expected to play a part will be okay with an alpha level of 5%.A good example of this is when we are investigating biology.

If a higher level of precision and accuracy is expected from the measuring instruments, then a low value of alpha can be used.

The p-values are normally set to between 0 and 1. If you find that the value of P is less than the cut-off that you chose, the null hypothesis should be rejected and the alternative hypothesis favored. However, if you find that P is greater than the cut-off, the

Chapter 3- Adjusted R-Squared

R-squared helps in measuring the proportion of variation in the dependent variable (Y) described by the independent variable (X) in linear regression. In adjusted R-squared, the statistic is adjusted based on the number of independent variables the model has. The R^2 normally shows how well the data points are fitting the curve. The adjusted R^2 also shows this, but in addition to this, it adjusts based on the number of terms the model has. In case more useless variables are added to the model, the adjusted R-squared will decrease. If more useful variables are added to the model, the adjusted R-squared ill increase.

The adjusted R^2_{adj} should be equal to or less than R^2. The R^2 is only required when you bare working with samples. This means that when you have data for the whole population, R^2 is not important for you. The adjusted R-squared is calculated using this formula:

$$R^2_{adj} = 1 - \left[\frac{\left(1 - R^2\right)(n - 1)}{n - k - 1} \right]$$

In which:

- N denotes the number of data points in the data sample.

- K refers to the number of independent regressors, that is, all variables in the model, minus the constant.

Example

The sample R-squared value for a particular fund is close to 0.5 and it is providing higher risk adjusted returns having a sample size of 100 for 10 predictors. Calculate the value for adjusted R-squared.

Solution:

Sample size = 100 Number of predictor = 10 Sample R - square = 0.5.

R2adj=1−[(1−0.5²)(100−1)/100−10−1]
= 1 - 0.83427
= 0.16573

Chapter 4- Analysis of Variance

This is also known as *ANOVA*. It refers to the steps that statisticians follow to determine the potential difference between scale-level dependent variable by nominal-level variable with two or more categories.

There are 3 different types of ANOVA. These include the following:

1. One-way ANOVA- these are made up of only one independent variable and it normally refers to the numbers in the variable. A good example of this is when you need to determine the difference in IQ between different countries. You may have data for 1, 2 and even more countries to compare.

2. Two-way ANOVA- this relies on two independent variables. A good example is when you need to determine the IQ difference between countries (this is variable 1) and between genders (variable 2). You are allowed to determine the interaction between two variables that are independent. For example, you may find that the females show a higher IQ compared to males, and that females in Europe and Asia have higher IQ than males.

• The two-way ANOVAs are also known as factorial ANOVA and they may be balanced or unbalanced. Balanced occurs when we have same number of participants in every group while in unbalanced, there are different number of participants in every group. The following are the methods that can be used to handle unbalanced ANOVAs:

• Hierarchical approach (Type 1) - this should be used when the data was not unbalanced willingly and the factors has some kind of hierarchy.

• Classical experimental approach (Type 2) - this should be used when the data was not unbalanced willingly and the factors don't have some kind of hierarchy.

• Full Regression approach (Type 3) - this should be applied when the data was unbalanced willingly due to the population.

3. Multivariate or N-way ANOVA- these are made up of a number of independent variables. Suppose you need to determine the difference in IQ by age, gender and country at once, you can deploy N-way ANOVA.

Steps for ANOVA Test

To carry out an ANOVA, follow the steps given below:

1. Create alternative and null hypothesis where null hypothesis should state that there isn't significant difference between the groups. In alternative hypothesis, there is an assumption that there is a significant difference between the groups.

2. Calculate the probability of F and the F-ratio.

3. Compare the p-value for the F-ratio with the determined significance level or alpha.

4. If F has a p-vale below 0.5, the null hypothesis should be rejected.

5. After the rejection of null hypothesis, it should be assumed that the groups don't have an equal mean.

Chapter 5- Calculating the Arithmetic Mean

The mean is the simplest and well known measure of central tendency. To calculate the mean of a dataset, we get the sum of the elements in the dataset then we divide by the number of items in the dataset. The mean is normally denoted as x-bar (x). The methods for calculating the arithmetic vary from one dataset to another depending on the series followed by the dataset.

Individual Data Series

We can calculate the mean for an individual data series. Here is an example of an individual data series:

10, 30, 45, 21, 43, 86, 34, 90, 67, 12

The above data shows a series of 20 data items. The mean for an individual data series may be calculated using this formula:

$$\overline{x} = \sum_{i=1}^{n} X_i$$

The formula can be written simply as follows:

$$\overline{x} = \frac{\sum x}{N}$$

Where:

- X_1, X_2, X_3 .... Are the individual observations in the variable?

- $\sum x$- refers to the sum of all the observations.

- N denotes the total number of observations.

Let us calculate the mean of the above 10 elements:

x = (10 + 30 + 45 + 21 + 43 + 86 + 34 + 90 + 67 + 12) / 10
= 438 / 10
= 43.8

The mean for the data is 43.8. Simply, you only have to get the sum of the elements then you divide it by the total number of elements that you have in the dataset.

Discrete Data Series

In a discrete data series, the data is given alongside the frequency with which it occurs. An example of such data is given below:

Item	10	30	21	43	86	34	90	67	12
Frequency	5	2	4	6	8	6	3	2	4

To calculate the mean for a data in a discrete series, we use the formula given below:

$$\bar{x} = \frac{f_1 x_1 + f_2 x_2 + f_3 x_3 \ldots + f_n x_n}{N}$$

The above formula can also be written as follows:

$$\bar{x} = \frac{\sum fx}{\sum f}$$

In which:

- N denotes the total number of observations.

- f1, f2, f3,...,fnf1, f2, f3,...,fn denotes the frequency for the different values.

- x1,x2,x3,...,xn denote the denote the different values for variable x.

Let us take our previous data and calculate its arithmetic mean. The data is as follows:

Item	10	30	21	43	86	34	90	67	12
Frequency	5	2	4	6	8	6	3	2	4

We can then create the following table from the above data:

Items	Frequency (f)	fx
10	5	50
30	2	60
21	4	84
43	6	258
86	8	688
34	6	204
90	3	270
67	2	134
12	4	48
	N = 40	$\sum fx$ = 1796

Hence:

x = 1796 / 40

= 44.9

This shows that the arithmetic mean for the above series is 44.9.

Continuous Data Series

This is the type of data in which we are given the data in ranges and their corresponding frequencies. Here is an example of such data:

Items	0-10	10-20	20-30	30-40	40-50
Frequency	2	5	4	6	2

The mean for such data can be calculated using the formula given below:

$$\bar{x} = \frac{f_1 m_1 + f_2 m_2 + f_3 m_3 \ldots\ldots + f_n m_n}{N}$$

In which:

- N denotes the number of observations.

- f_1, f_2, f_3,..., f_n denote the different values of frequency f.

- m_1, m_2, m_3,..., m_n denotes the different values for the midpoints for the ranges.

Let us calculate the arithmetic mean for the above data. From the data, we can create the following table:

Items	Mid-points (m)	Frequency (f)	fm
0 − 5	5	2	10
10 − 20	15	5	75
20 − 30	25	4	100
30 − 40	35	6	210
40 - 50	45	2	90
		N = 19	Σfm = 485

From the above data, the arithmetic can be calculated as follows:

x = 485 / 19
= 25.53

Hence, the arithmetic mean for our dataset is 25.53.

Chapter 6- Arithmetic Median

Arithmetic median denotes the positional average and it is the middle value in a particular data distribution. To find the media of a dataset, the items in the dataset should first be arranged in an ascending or descending order. After that, the data is divided into two halves and the element at the middle is identified. This element is identified as M for median.

The process of calculating the median of a data series is also different and is determined by the type of series for the dataset. Let us discuss how this can be calculated for the various types of data series.

Individual Series

Here is an example of data in an individual series:

10, 30, 45, 21, 43, 86, 34, 90, 67, 12

If the dataset has an even number of distribution, the values should first be arranged in an ascending order then get the arithmetic mean of the two values at the middle. This will give the median for the distribution.

Median = Value of the $(N+1/2)^{th}$ item.

In which N denotes the number of observations in the distribution.

If we have the following distribution given previously:

10, 30, 45, 21, 43, 86, 34, 90, 67, 12

Solution:

Let us first arrange the data in ascending order:

10, 12, 21, 30, 34, 43, 45, 67, 86, 90

Median = Value of the (N+1/2)th item.

= (10 + 1) / 2
= Value of 5.5th item
= value of (5th item + 6th item) / 2
= (34 + 43) / 2
= 38.5

This shows that the arithmetic mean for the distribution is 38.5.

Note that we followed the above steps because the distribution has an even number of items. If we had an odd number of items, then we can easily pick the item at the middle of all after arranging them in an ascending order. Suppose you have the following distribution:

7, 35, 13, 24, 1

We have a total of 5 items in the distribution. First, let us arrange them in an ascending order: 1, 7, 13, 24, 35

From the above, we can easily pick 13 as the number at the middle of the data. This means that 13 is the arithmetic median of the data.

Discrete Series

This is the kind of data that is given together with the frequency of occurrence of the various elements in the dataset. Here is an example of such data:

Item	10	30	21	43	86	34	90	67	12
Frequency	5	2	4	6	8	6	3	2	4

We have just used the data that we had previously. If the group has an even number of distribution, the arithmetic median can be calculated by taking the arithmetic mean of the two values at the middle of the data once the data items have been arranged in an ascending order. It is calculated using this formula:

Median = Value of the $(N+1/2)^{\text{th}}$ item.

In which:

N denotes the total number of observations.

Let us calculate the arithmetic median for the data given above:

First, we arrange the data in ascending order:

Median = Value of the (N+1/2)ᵗʰ item.

10, 12, 21, 30, 34, 43, 45, 67, 86, 90
= (34 + 43) / 2

= 38.5

This means that the value of the median for the above distribution is 38.5.

Note that we followed the above steps because the distribution has an even number of items. If we had an odd number of items, then we can easily pick the item at the middle of all after arranging them in an ascending order.

Suppose you have the following distribution:

7, 35, 13, 24, 1

We have a total of 5 items in the distribution. First, let us arrange them in an ascending order:

1, 7, 13, 24, 35

From the above, we can easily pick 13 as the number at the middle of the data. This means that 13 is the arithmetic median of the data.

Continuous Series

Items	0-10	10-20	20-30	30-40	40-50
Frequency	2	5	4	6	2

A continuous series has made in ranges together with the frequencies. Consider the following example. The median for such data can be calculated using the formula given below:

$$Median = L + \frac{(\frac{n}{2} - c.f.)}{f} \times i$$

In which:

- L denotes the lower limit for the median class, and the median class is the class in which the n/2th item lies.

- c.f. denotes the cumulative frequency for the class that precedes the median class.

- f denotes the frequency for the median class.

- i denotes the class interval for the median class.

The arithmetic median becomes a very useful measure of central tendency when we have a nominal data.

Since the arithmetic median is a positional average, it is not affected by any extreme values in the data.

Example:

The following table shows the monthly pay of workers in a particular company. The data shows the number of employees whose monthly is between a particular range.

Salary Range ($):

1) 0-500 (Number of Employees: 6)
2) 500-1000 (Number of Employees: 7)
3) 1000-1500 (Number of Employees: 9)
4) 1500-2000 (Number of Employees: 8)
5) 2000-2500 (Number of Employees: 4)
6) 2500-300 (Number of Employees: 6)

We can calculate the median for the above data. We can calculate the cumulative frequency and other details for the data as shown below:

Salary Range:

1) 0 – 500 (Mi point: 250, Frequency (f): 6, (m-1250)/500d: -2, fd: 12, c.f: 6)

2) 500 – 1000 (Mi point: 750, Frequency (f): 7, (m-1250)/500d: -1, fd: 7, c.f: 3)

3) 1000 – 1500 (Mi point: 1250, Frequency (f): 9, (m-1250)/500d: 0, fd: 0, c.f: 2)

4) 1500 - 2000(Mi point: 1750, Frequency (f): 8, (m-1250)/500d: 1, fd: 8, c.f: 0)

5) 2000 – 2500 (Mi point: 2250, Frequency (f): 4, (m-1250)/500d: 2, fd: 8, c.f: 4)

6) 2500 – 3000 (Mi point: 2750, Frequency (f): 6, (m-1250)/500d: 3, fd: 8, c.f: 0)

N = 40
$\sum$ fd = 15

What happened is that we chose a common factor as 500, that is, i = 500.

We can then use the following formula to determine the median salary for the employees in the company:

$$Median = L + \frac{(\frac{n}{2} - c.f.)}{f} \times i$$

The following are the values for the various elements in the above formula:

- L = 1000
- c.f = 13

- n/2 = 20
- f = 9
- i = 500

Median = 1 + [(20 − 13) / 9] * 500
= 1000 + 388.9
= 1388.9

This means that the median wage for the employees in the company is 1388.9 which are approximately 1389.

Chapter 7- Arithmetic Mode

The mode is the item that occurs most frequently within a dataset. This means that the mode item is the one with the highest frequency. The calculation of mode is determined by the type of data series that you have. Let us discuss how this calculated for various data series:

Individual Series

When given data that is in an individual series, you just have to count the number of times that each time occurs. The item that occurs many times is the mode for the data. Consider the example data series given below:

1, 3, 7, 5, 3, 2, 4, 3, 2, 9

After counting the number of times each element occurs, we find that 3 have the highest frequency of 3. This makes it the modal value for the dataset.

Discrete Series

In this type of data series, the data is given together with the frequency of occurrence of the items. In discrete series data, the modal for the data can be obtained by inspecting and finding the item with the highest frequency associated with it. However, in some cases, the difference between the frequency with the highest value and the one succeeding or preceding it may be too small.

In such a case, it is recommended that you use the grouping table method to find the modal value for the data series.

Consider the following table showing the various elements and the corresponding frequency of their occurrence:

Item	10	30	21	43	86	34	90	67	12
Frequency	5	2	4	6	12	6	3	2	4

From the table above, it is very clear that the highest frequency is 12, associated with the item 86. This means that 86 is the mode for the data.

Continuous Series

A continuous data is given in ranges and their associated frequencies. The following formula is used to calculate the mode of a continuous data:

$$M_0 = L + \frac{f_1 - f_0}{2f_1 - f_0 - f_2} \times i$$

Whereby:

- Mo is the Mode
- f1 is the frequency of the modal class

- f0 is the frequency of the pre-modal class
- f2 is the Frequency of the class succeeding the modal class
- i is the Class interval.

In case we find that there are two variable values with highest frequency, it means that the series is bimodal and the mode is termed as ill-defined. In such a case, we can use the following formula to calculate the value of the mode:

Mode = 3 Median - 2 Mean

The arithmetic mode is a good way of describing qualitative phenomenon such as brand preference, consumer preferences etc. It can be used even in cases when we don't have a normal data. The reason is that it is not affected by any extreme values in the data.

Consider the data given below:

Salary	No. of Employees
0 − 5	3
5 − 10	7
10 − 15	15
15 - 20	30
20 - 25	20
25 - 30	10
30 - 35	5

We can use the formula given below to calculate the mode of the data:

$$M_0 = L + \frac{f_1 - f_0}{2f_1 - f_0 - f_2} \times i$$

From the above data, the following are the values of the various elements of the formula:

- $f_0 = 15$
- $f_1 = 30$
- $f_2 = 20$
- $L = 15$
- $i = 5$

Substituting the respective values in the formula, we end up with the following:

Mode = 15 +3
= 18

This means that the mode for the data series is 18.

Chapter 8- Arithmetic Range

The arithmetic range for a dataset is calculated by getting the difference between the highest and lowest values in a dataset. The following formula is used for calculating the arithmetic range for a particular dataset:

Range=L–S

In which:

- L denotes the largest element.
- S denotes the smallest element.

The above formula gives us an absolute measure. To get the relative measure, commonly known as the *coefficient of range*, we use the formula given below:

Coefficient of Range = (L-S) / (L + S)

Example:

The following data shows the scores made by a student in statistic tests:

89, 84, 91, 73, 87, 94, 77

Use the above data to calculate the range of his test score and the coefficient of range.

Solution:

First, let us arrange the scores in an ascending order, from the least to the largest:

73   77   84   87   89   91   94

The Range is calculated as follows:

Range = Largest − Smallest
= 94 − 73
= 21
Largest + Smallest
= 94 + 73
= 167

The coefficient of range can be calculated using this formula:

Coefficient of Range = (L-S) / (L + S)
Coefficient of Range = 21/167

= 0.1257

From the above calculations, it is clear that the scores have a range of 21 and the range of coefficient is 0.1257.

Chapter 9- Point Estimation

Point estimation refers to use of sample data to determine a single value referred to as a *statistic* that will serve as the "best estimate" or "best guess" for the unknown parameter of the population. Formally, it is the application of point estimate to some data.

To calculate the Best point, we first begin by calculating the value for Maximum Likelihood Estimation (MLE) using the following formula:

MLE = S/T

Next, we calculate the value for Laplace using the following formula:

$$Laplace = \frac{S + 1}{T + 2}$$

Next, we calculate the value for Jeffrey using the following formula:

$$Jeffrey = \frac{S + 0.5}{T + 1}$$

Lastly, we calculate the value of Wilson using the following formula:

$$Wilson = \frac{S + \dfrac{z^2}{2}}{T + z^2}$$

In which:

- MLE is the Maximum Likelihood Estimation
- SS is the Number of Success
- T is the Number of trials
- Z is the Z-Critical Value

When doing Best Point Estimation, follow the rules given below:

1. MLE<=0.5 -Wilson Estimation
2. Between MLE>0.5 and MLE<0.9 - MLE
3. MLE>0.9 - either Jeffrey or Laplace depending on which is small.

Example:

Suppose a coin is tossed 4 times in 9 trials at 99% confidence interval, determine the best point for success of the coin.

Solution:

From the above description, we can get values for the following parameters:
Success(S) = 4

Trials (T) = 9
Confidence Interval Level (P) = 99% = 0.99

For us to calculate the best point estimation, we should first calculate all the values as shown below:

MLE = S/T
= 4/9
= 0.4444

Next, we use the formula for Laplace:

Laplace = (4 + 1) / (9 + 2)
= 5 / 11
= 0.4545

Next, we can use the formula for Jeffrey as follows:

= (4 + 0.5) / (9 + 1)
= 4.5 / 10
= 0.45

You can now use the Z table to determine the Z-critical value.

The Z-critical value for 99% level is 2.5758.

We can then use the formula for Wilson and substitute the respective values as follows:

[4+(2.5758 / 2)^2 / 2] / [9+2.5758$2^{2]}$

= 0.468

From the above calculation, the MLE ≤ 0.5, hence the Best Point Estimate will be 0.468.

Chapter 10- Calculating Skewness

Dispersion is normally used to measure the amount of variation. Skewness is used for measuring the direction of variation. Skewness is normally measured in Karl Pearson's measure, which is commonly written with the symbol Skp. It can be seen as a relative measure for skewness.

Skewness normally represents asymmetry and imbalance from the mean of data distribution. Skewness is normally calculated using the following formula:

skewness = (3 * (mean - median)) / standard deviation

In a symmetrical distribution, the value for the coefficient of skewness is zero since there will be a coincidence between the mea, the mode and the median. If this coefficient has a positive value, the distribution is skewed positively while if it has a negative value, the coefficient is skewed negatively.

Skewness can be expressed as follows in terms of moments:

$$\beta_1 = \frac{\mu_3^2}{\mu_2^2}$$

In which:

$$\mu_3 = [\sum(X - x)^3]/N$$

and:

$$\mu_2 = [\sum(X - x)^2]/N$$

If you find that μ_3 has value of zero, this is an indication that the distribution is symmetrical. A higher value of μ_3 is an indication that there is a higher symmetry. However, from the μ_3, we are unable to tell the direction of skewness.

Example:

The following table shows data collected about the strength of engineering students in two different colleges:

Measure	College X	College Y
Mean	151	146
Median	142	153
S. deviation	30	30

Are the two distributions similar in their variation?

Solution:

From the above data, we can easily tell that the two colleges have an equal number of students. However, we are unable to tell whether the two distributions are similar.

Due to this, a further analysis is needed by determining the value of skewness. Here is the formula for calculating skewness:

skewness = (3 * (mean - median)) / standard deviation

We are not given the value of mode, but we can use the following formula to calculate it:

Mode=3Median−2Mean

The mode for college X can be calculated as follows:

Mode=3(142)−2(151)
= 426 − 302
= 124

The skewness can then be calculated as follows:

= (151 − 124) / 30
= 27 / 30
= 0.9

The mode for college Y can be calculated as follows:

Mode=3(153) − 2(146)
= 459 − 292
= 167

The skewness can then be calculated as follows:

= (143 − 167) / 30

= -24 / 30
= -0.8

That is how skewness can be calculated for a distribution.

Example 2:

Suppose we have the data given below representing observations:

{12, 13, 25, 54, 56}

Calculate the skewness of the above data.

Solution:

The first step should involve calculating the mean and the standard deviation of the data.

The mean can be calculated by getting the sum of the elements and dividing by 5 as follows:

12 + 13 + 25 + 54 + 56 = 160
= 160 / 5
= 32

The calculation of standard deviation requires us to subtract the mean from the value of an item then square it.

The square root of their sum will be the standard deviation. This can be calculated as follows:

$S^2 = \{(12 - 32)^2 + (13 - 32)^2 + (25 - 32)^2 + (54 - 32)^2 + (56 - 32)^2 \}/5 = 374$
$S = 374^{1/2} = 19.34$

We can then go ahead to calculate the value of skewness using the following formula:

$S_k = \{ \Sigma(X_i - X)^3\}/s^3 * 1/n$
$= \{(12 - 32)^3 + (13 - 32)^3 + (25 - 32)^3 + (54 - 32)^3 + (56 - 32)^3 \} /19.34^3 * 1/5$
$= 0.256$

The value for skewness is positive. This means that the above data has a positively skewed distribution.

Chapter 11- Kurtosis

Kurtosis is used to measure the degree of peakedness or flatness. It tells us the extent to which the distribution is peak or flat compared to the normal curve. With kurtosis, we can show three different curves in a diagram.

These are the mesokurtic curve, which is the normal curve. In this type of distribution, the kurtosis statistic is similar to the one for a normal distribution. Which means that the distribution has an extreme value characteristic that is similar to the one for a normal distribution?

There is also the leptokurtic curve, which is when a distribution is more peaked compared to the normal or the mesokurtic curve. This means the distribution has a more kurtosis compared to a normal distribution. This type of distribution is characterized by outliers, which are long tails. The outliers give the leptokurtic distribution skinniness, making easy to remember it. Some individuals classify the leptokurtic distribution as being distributed towards the mean. However, the most things to note about this type of distribution are that there are outliers that give it its shape.

Lastly we have the platykurtic curve, which is when the distribution is less peaked compared to the normal or mesokurtic curve. This type of distribution is characterized by short tails.

Kurtosis is determined using the following formula:

$$\beta_2 = \frac{\mu_4}{\mu_2}$$

Whereby:

$\mu_4 = \Sigma(x - x)^4 / N$

A higher value for \beta_2 means that the distribution will be more peaked, giving a leptokurtic curve. If the curve is normal, it has a value of 3, if it is leptokurtic, its value is greater than 3 while if it is platykurtic, and its value is less than 3.

Example:

Calculate the type of kurtosis exhibited by the following data:

(12, 13, 25, 54, 56)

Solution:

The first step should involve calculating the mean and the standard deviation of the data. The mean can be calculated by getting the sum of the elements and dividing by 5 as follows:

12 + 13 + 25 + 54 + 56 = 160
= 160 / 5 = 32

The calculation of standard deviation requires us to subtract the mean from the value of an item then square it. The square root of their sum will be the standard deviation. This can be calculated as follows:

$$S^2 = \{(12 - 32)^2 + (13 - 32)^2 + (25 - 32)^2 + (54 - 32)^2 + (56 - 32)^2\} / 5 = 374$$
$$S = 374^{1/2} = 19.34$$

Now we have the values for the mean and the standard deviation. We can apply our formula straight to get the value for kurtosis.

$$\mathbf{S_{kr} = \{(12 - 32)^4 + (13 - 32)^4 + (25 - 32)^4 + (54 - 32)^4 + (56 - 32)^4 / 19.34^4 * 1/5 = 1.228}$$

Remember that we said a normal kurtosis has a value of 3. Since we have the value for kurtosis, we can subtract 3 from it to know the real value. This will help us know the type of kurtosis exhibited by the data.

The excess kurtosis can be calculated as follows:

$$1.228 - 3 = -1.772$$

The value for the excess kurtosis is a negative number. Due to this, we can conclude that our data has a platykurtic kurtosis.

Chapter 12- Linear Regression

Correlation analysis is a good way of determining the relationship between variables. Once this relationship have been determined, it is always good to go further to determine the degree of the relationship between the variables. Linear regression can help us achieve this. It helps us know the cause and effect relationship between the variables that we have. We are only required to know the relationship between the dependent and independent variable. This normally leads to an algebraic equation or a graph. From these, we can determine the values of dependent variables when the value of the independent variable is known.

Graphs

The graphical method normally involves drawing of a scatter diagram with the independent variable on the X-axis while the dependent variable on the Y-axis. A line is than fitted in such a way that it passes where there is majority of the distribution. The rest of the points are left distributed evenly on both sides of the line.

The regression line is normally referred to as the *line of best fit* as it summarizes the movement of data generally.
It shows the best mean values for a variable that correspond to the mean value for the other variable. The line of best is normally drawn using the criteria that it will minimize the sum of the squared deviations between observed and predicted values for a dependent variable.

Algebraic Equation

With this method, we develop two regression equations for Y on X and X on Y. The regression equation for Y on X should be as shown below:

Y=a+bX

Whereby:

- Y is the dependent variable.
- X is the independent variable.
- a is a constant showing the Y-intercept.
- b is a constant showing the slope of the line.

The following normal equations can be used for calculating the values of a and b:

$$\sum Y = Na + b\sum X$$

$$\sum XY = a\sum X + b\sum X^2$$

Whereby N denotes the total number of observations.

The regression equation for X on Y is as follows:

X=a+bY

Whereby:

- X is the dependent variable.

- Y is the independent variable.
- a is a constant showing the Y-intercept.
- b is a constant showing the slope of the line.

The normal equations given below can be used to calculate the values for a and b:

$$\sum X = Na + b\sum Y$$
$$\sum XY = a\sum Y + b\sum Y^2$$

Where N denotes the total number of observations.

Consider the following data in a table:

x	y
1	1
2	3
4	3
3	2
5	5

The data shows the different values for variable x and the corresponding values for variable y.

The x is the independent variable while y is the dependent variable that we need to predict. If we get additional data, we will only be able to get the values of x then use then to get/predict the corresponding values for y. If a graph of y against x is plotted for the above data, it will be found that the relationship between x and y is kind of linear.

This means that we are able to draw a line running diagonally from the bottom left corner of the graph to the top right corner. This shows that linear regression can be applied for that small data set.

When we are having a single input variable x and we need to use linear regression, then it is referred to as *simple linear regression*. If we are having several input variables, x1, x2, x3 etc. we refer to it as *multiple linear regression*. Linear regression has a simple procedure compared to multiple linear regressions, making it good for beginners.

We can create a linear regression equation from the above data. We will then be able to use this equation to make predictions.

The data will be modeled as follows:

Y = a + bX

The y above is the dependent variable that we need to predict, while x is the independent variable that we know. The a and b are the coefficients that will move the line around and we need to estimate them. The coefficient a is known as the intercept since it will determine where the line will intercept the y-axis. In machine learning, it is known as the bias since it will be added for the purpose of offsetting all the predictions that we make.

The term b is known as the slope since it will define the slope of the line, that is, how x is translated into y before the bias can be added.

We need to get the best estimates for the coefficients to minimize the errors when we are predicting the value of y from x.

The value of b can be estimated as follows:

b = sum((xi-mean(x)) * (yi-mean(y))) / sum((xi − mean(x))^2)

The *mean()* is the average value for variable in the dataset. The use of xi and yi denotes that we are in need of repeating these calculations across all the values in the dataset and the i refers to the i'th value for x and y.

To calculate a, we can use b and the statistics from the dataset as shown below:

a = mean(y) − b * mean(x)

Slope Estimation (b)

We can begin with the numerator, which is the top part of the equation. We should first get the mean value for x and y. We use this formula to get the mean:

1/n * sum(x)

In our case, we have 5 values, hence n is 5. If you have the data in excel, you can call the AVERAGE() function and get the mean. The mean for x is 3 while the mean for y is 2.8.

To get the mean for x, add all values for x then divide by 5. To get the mean for y, add the values for y then divide by 5:

Mean (x) = (1+ 2+ 4+ 3 +5)/3 = 3
Mean (y) = (1 +3 +3 +2 +5)/5 = 2.8

From the above means, we are able to get the error for every variable. To do this, we use the following formula:

For x:
x- mean(x)
For y:
y − mean (y)

We can demonstrate this in a table as follows:

x	mean (x)	X − mean(x)
1	3	-2
2	3	-1
4	3	1
3	3	0
5	3	2

We can do the same for y:

y	mean (y)	y – mean(y)
1	2.8	-1.8
3	2.8	0.2
3	2.8	0.2
2	2.8	-0.8
5	2.8	2.2

All the parts that can be used for calculation of the numerator are now ready. We should multiple the errors for each x with the corresponding error for each y then get the sum for these multiplications:

Mean (x)	Mean (y)	Multiplication
-2	-1.8	3.6
-1	0.2	-0.2
1	0.2	0.2
0	-0.8	0
2	2.2	4.4

Get the sum of the final column, that is, Multiplication. It will be equal to 8 and this is the numerator. We should now get the denominator, which is the bottom part of the equation for calculation of b. This involves getting the sum of squared differences for every value of x from the mean. We already have the difference for each value if x from the mean, so now we should square them then get their sum.

x – mean (x)	Squared
-2	4
-1	1

1	1
0	0
2	4

After getting the sum of the squared values, we get 10, which is the value for the denominator. We can now get the value for the slope:

b = 8/10
b = 0.8

Getting the Intercept (a)

We are now aware of all the values that are needed, making this easy for us:

a = mean(y) – b * mean(x)
a = 2.8 – 0.8 * 3
b = 0.4

You now have it!

Now that we have the coefficients for the simple linear regression equation, we can use it to make predictions. The equation with the coefficients is as follows:

Y = a + b * X
Y = 0.4 + 0.8 * X

We can now use our previous training data to make predictions for the value of y:

x	y	Predicted y
1	1	1.2
2	3	2
4	3	3.6
3	2	2.8
5	5	4.4

If you plot a graph of y against x for the predicted values of y, you will get a diagonal line cutting through all the points. This shows how the lines model the data.

Error Estimation

We can now get the error for the values that we have predicted. This will be the Root Mean Squared Error (RMSE). We should this formula to get the RMSE:

RMSE = sqrt(sum((pi − yi)^2)/n)

The sqrt() represents the square root function, p is the value that we predicted while y is the actual value, i represents the index for the instance, n denotes the number of predictions since we should get the error for all the predicted values. We should first get the difference between every model prediction and actual values for y.

This is shown below:

Predicted y	y	Error
1.2	1	0.2
2	3	-1
3.6	3	0.6
2.8	2	0.8
4.4	5	-0.6

You can then square the values of the error given above, that is, *error * error* or *error^2.*

The sum of the errors is 2.4 units. To get the value of RMSE, we can divide it by n then get the square root to give us the following:

RMSE = 0.692

This means that very prediction that we make has an average error of around 0.692 units.

Other than having to follow all the above steps, there is a shortcut you can use to get to the values of a and b. The b can be calculated using this formula:

b = corr(x, y) * stdev(y) / stdev(x)

The corr(x) denotes the correlation between x and y, while the stdev() denotes the standard deviation for the variable. Correlation is used to measure the relationship between two variables in a range of -1 to 1. If the value is

1, it means that the two variables are positively and perfectly correlated, meaning that if one moves, the other one moves in the other direction.

Standard deviation measures how much on average a data is spread from the mean.

Chapter 13- Binomial Distribution

The binomial distribution is normally used in cases where an experiment gives two possibilities, a success and a failure. It is a discrete probability distribution that expresses a set of two alternative successes (p) and the failures (q). The following probability function defines binomial distribution:

$$P(X-x) = {}^nC_x Q^{n-x} . p^x$$

Whereby:

- p is the probability of success.
- Q is y the probability of failure, that is, $1-p$.
- N is the number of trials.
- $P(X-x)$ is the probability of achieving x successes for n trials.

Example 1:

Suppose a test with multiple choice questions is conducted. Each question has 4 choices for the answers, out of which only one of them is correct. Calculate the probability that a person who undertakes the test scores 5 questions wrong.

Solution:

From the above information, the following are the values for the various variables:

n = 20,
n - k = 5,
k = 20 - 5 = 15

The probability of giving the right answer is the probability of success, s = ¼ - we have 4 options for answer per question.

The probability of failure is simply the probability of giving wrong answer, which is, 1 −s, which is, 1 − ¼ = ¾

The above can then be substituted in the formula for calculating the binomial distribution to give the following:

P (probability of getting 5 incorrect answers out of 20) =
C (20, 5) * (14) ^{15} * (3/4)^5
P = [(20*19*18*17*16)/ (5*4*3*2*1)] * (1/4)^{15} * (3/4)^5
= 0.0000034

This means that we need a probability of approximately 0.0000034.

Conclusion

This marks the end of this guide. With statistics, we can unearth the hidden meaning of a dataset. There are various measures that we can calculate about our data. These measures are very informative whenever we need to determine the relationship between the various data variables. Examples of such are the measures of central tendency which include the mean, the mode and the median. The mean is a good measure as it tells us how the data is distributed. The mode tells us about the item with the highest frequency in the dataset. This is the item that occurs most frequently. The median tells us the item that is at the middle or center of the data. The calculation of these measures is determined by the kind of data in question. The data may be in individual series, discrete series or in a continuous series. Once the relationship between the various variables in the dataset has been established, it becomes easy to make predictions for unknown values. With statistics, we can determine the most correct value that can be used to fill in the missing values in a dataset.